States of Matter
# Mass

by Rebecca Pettiford

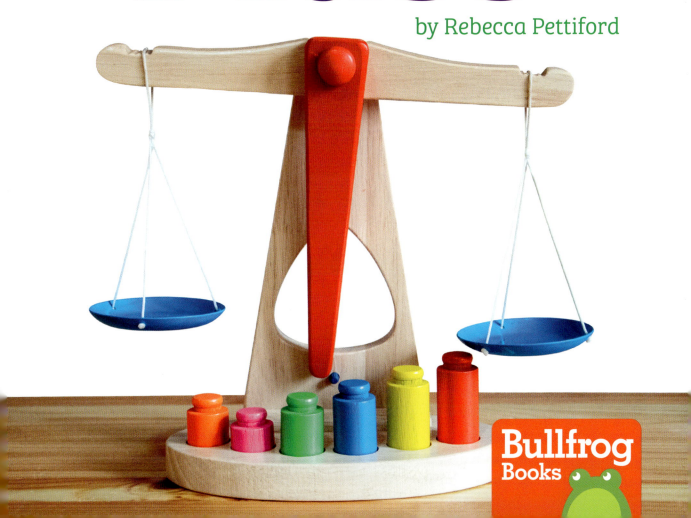

Bullfrog Books

# Ideas for Parents and Teachers

Bullfrog Books let children practice reading informational text at the earliest reading levels. Repetition, familiar words, and photo labels support early readers.

## Before Reading
- Discuss the cover photo. What does it tell them?
- Look at the picture glossary together. Read and discuss the words.

## During Reading
- "Walk" through the book with the reader. Discuss new or unfamiliar words. Sound them out together.
- Look at the photos together. Point out the photo labels.

## After Reading
- Prompt the child to think more. Ask: Mass is how much matter is in something. What more would you like to learn about matter?

Bullfrog Books are published by Jump!
5357 Penn Avenue South
Minneapolis, MN 55419
www.jumplibrary.com

Copyright © 2026 Jump! International copyright reserved in all countries. No part of this book may be reproduced in any form without written permission from the publisher.

Jump! is a division of FlutterBee Education Group.

Library of Congress Cataloging-in-Publication Data is available at www.loc.gov or upon request from the publisher.

ISBN: 979-8-89213-963-2 (hardcover)
ISBN: 979-8-89213-964-9 (paperback)
ISBN: 979-8-89213-965-6 (ebook)

Editor: Jenna Gleisner
Designer: Anna Peterson

Photo Credits: Ioannis Pantzi/Shutterstock, cover; tilimili13/Shutterstock, 1; EVGEIIA/Shutterstock, 3; Tom Merton/iStock, 4, 5 (left); Paulus Rusyanto/Dreamstime, 5 (right); Vizerskaya/iStock, 5 (background); AndyElliott/Shutterstock, 6–7; Tran Van Quyet/iStock, 8–9, 23bl; Hseena/Shutterstock, 10; Tiplyashina Evgeniya/Shutterstock, 11, 12–13; aperturesound/Shutterstock, 14; solidcolours/iStock, 15, 23tr; Lightfieldstudiosprod/Dreamstime, 16–17; Victor Moussa/Shutterstock, 18–19, 20–21, 23tl, 23br (scale); HAKINMHAN/Shutterstock, 18–19, 20–21, 23tl, 23br (background); Sony Herdiana/Shutterstock, 20–21, 23br (pickleball); Dionisvera/Shutterstock, 20–21, 23br (apple); MerlinTmb/Shutterstock, 22 (yarn); Artem Stepanov/Shutterstock, 22 (balloons); TatianaMishina/Shutterstock, 24.

Printed in the United States of America at Corporate Graphics in North Mankato, Minnesota.

# Table of Contents

| | |
|---|---|
| Mass and Matter | 4 |
| Air and Mass | 22 |
| Picture Glossary | 23 |
| Index | 24 |
| To Learn More | 24 |

# Mass and Matter

Can you move a flower?
Yes!

# Can you move an elephant?

No!

Why?

It has too much **mass**.

Everything is made of **matter**.

Even you!

Mass is the amount of matter in something.

# One box is empty.

## Another is full.

Which has more mass?
The box full of kittens!
Why?
It has more matter in it.

# One balloon is empty.

Another is full.
It has air in it.

Which has more mass?
The one with air in it!

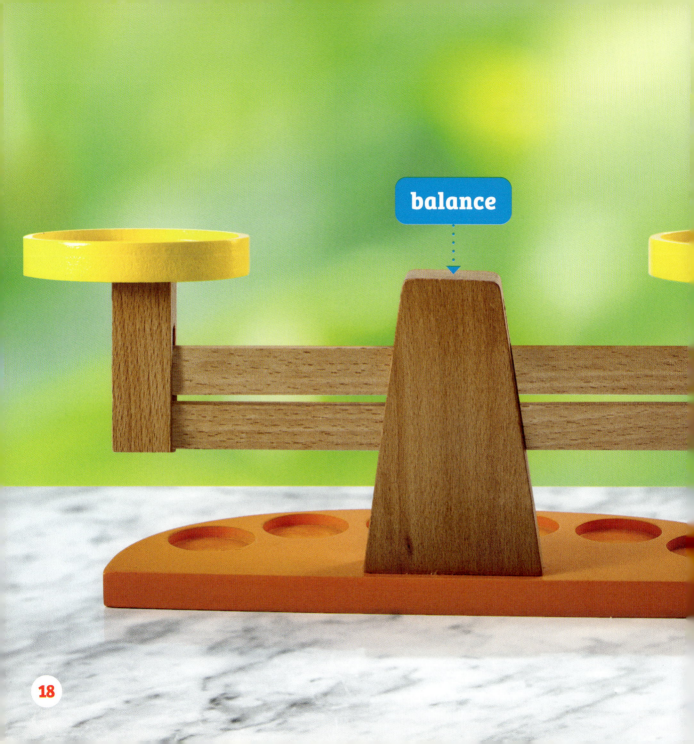

We can **measure** mass.

How?

We use a **balance**.

Which has more mass?

The balance tips.

The apple does!

# Air and Mass

Which balloon has more mass? Let's experiment and see!

**What You Need:**
- two of the same kind of balloon
- a wood stick like a chopstick or a ruler
- scissors
- string
- tape

**Steps:**
1. Cut one piece of string. Tie it to the center of the stick.
2. Tape one empty balloon to one end of the stick.
3. Tape the other empty balloon to the other end of the stick.
4. Tie the string around a door or drawer handle so it hangs. The stick should be level, or straight across. Why? Each empty balloon has the same mass.
5. Take one balloon off. Blow it up with air. Tie the balloon, and tape it back to the stick. Watch what happens.

The balloon with air has more mass! Why? It is filled with air and more matter!

# Picture Glossary

### balance
A device for weighing things or comparing the weight of objects.

### mass
The amount of physical matter that an object has inside it.

### matter
Something that has weight and takes up space, such as a solid, liquid, or gas.

### measure
To find the size, weight, or amount of something.

# Index

apple 20
balance 19, 20
balloon 14
box 10, 12
elephant 5
empty 10, 14
flower 4
full 11, 12, 15
kittens 12
matter 9, 12
measure 19
move 4, 5

# To Learn More

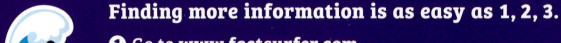

**Finding more information is as easy as 1, 2, 3.**

❶ Go to www.factsurfer.com

❷ Enter "**mass**" into the search box.

❸ Choose your book to see a list of websites.